The Heart of Newfoundland

Stanley Burke
Peggie Coulter

Stone House

Stone House Publishing Inc.
P.O. Box 9301, Stn., A,
Halifax, Nova Scotia, Canada, B3K 5N5

Canadian Cataloguing in Publication Data
Burke, Stanley, 1923-
    The Heart of Newfoundland
    ISBN 0-921128-30-4

1. Newfoundland – Description and travel – 1981 –
Views. I. Coulter, Peggie, 1933- II. Title.

FC2167.5.B87 1990   971,8'04'022   C89-098687-8
F1122.B87 1990

Printed and bound in Singapore

Special thanks to Don Morgan, Creative Publishers, St. John's.

ISBN 0-921128-30-4

DEDICATION

To the open hearts of Newfoundland
where we have been welcomed as
nowhere else.

Stanley Burke

Peggie Coulter

CONTENTS

The Heart of Newfoundland

An island ablaze with wildflowers; communities bright with colour, more colour than anywhere else in Canada; and the warmest-hearted people in the world.

This is Newfoundland.

It is a fierce and storm-lashed island, of course, where people for centuries struggled to survive — but they also knew how to celebrate.

Doors were always open, no one knocked. Help and laughter were always close at hand.

Often, they danced until dawn in one another's homes. They created songs and stories and loved practical jokes — even at wakes and funerals.

They made the most out of what was at hand — whether in building a boat, feeding a family, or celebrating a wedding.

Life was hard but full of colour and heart.

This heritage is alive today. Doors are still open and hospitality is a way of life. If you move to an outport, as we did, neighbours come smiling through your door bringing gifts of fresh-caught cod, a piece of moose shot yesterday, or simply to say "ye'll be welcome."

Our telephone man, having fixed our phone, stayed at the end of the day to give us a folksong concert and a guitar lesson — and to become a friend. When our car went into a ditch, eight men appeared from nowhere to lift us out and a mishap became a colourful social occasion.

Warmth is everywhere, in people and in nature.

Skies are the most dramatic we have seen and, as a fellow-photographer said, "All you need do is look up."

Sun filters through drifting fog creating a muted glow over the landscape.

Storm-driven waves strike the cliffs and explode a hundred feet in the air.

Irridescent icebergs sail by like flotillas of frozen galleons.

Even the rocks bloom with flowers and berries.

And, everywhere, laughing laundry dances in the wind beside friendly homes.

Newfoundland is bright with colour, warm with emotion, and this book is dedicated to the people who make it that way — the Warmest Hearted People In The World.

THE WARMEST
HEARTED PEOPLE

IN THE WORLD

4

WOOMP! This one is going 120 feet in the air drowning an entire island! Fishermen told us these were the biggest waves in 10 years.

GOTCHA! This rogue wave made a grab for Peggie. If she had gone into that cauldron, survival chances were just about zero.

SEEING THE LIGHT

Visiting lighthouses is one of New-foundland's special pleasures. The lightkeepers, like most Newfoundlanders, are hospitable and have a fund of stories. They offered us tea, dinner, tales of peril and bravery, and even a bed for the night.

The light mechanisms in older lighthouses are masterpieces of 19th century English workmanship with clockwork systems, no longer in use, which once rotated the giant prisms. Every piece which went into the building of lighthouses had to be landed through surf from ships.

OUTPORTS — Where strangers are welcomed as family — "It's the Proper Thing!"

RED BOATS AND WARM HEARTS

The west coast outport of Trout River, is famous for fishing and friendliness. Brightly-coloured boats seem to reflect the warmth of the reception we received there, a welcome which included dinners of fresh salmon and roast moose in a century-old house.

SALTFISH AND
SCARE-GULLS

Ed Power and son Francis make saltfish in the beautiful outport of Brigus South. Small and protected, it is a delight for photographers and movie makers. The 'scare-gull', hanging above the flake, ensures that the Powers will eat the cod, not unwanted winged visitors. The village ducks are frightened by nothing.

TRANQUIL TRINITY — This post card-perfect outport once rivalled St. John's, producing more wealth than all French Canada. Probably the oldest permanent settlement in Newfoundland, it was the site of the first court of justice in the New World north of Mexico. Today, it is a tourist delight often called the "Williamsburg' of Newfoundland.

MILLION-YEAR-OLD ICE-CUBES — Aboard a 64-year-old tug, we sailed from Twillingate to Labrador through bergy waters, as they are called in the marine forecasts. We pulled in a 'bergy bit', or 'growler', and celebrated the occasion with a million-year toast.

Don't let a good catch be your last reward.

FOR THE LOVE OF COD

Sixty-four year old tug *Deer Lake* returns to her home port, Corner Brook, on her last Newfoundland voyage.

COD QUEENS AND UNCLE IGGY — A highlight of many summer celebrations is choosing the Cod Queen from the workers at local fish plants. Fishing is also a pleasure and Uncle Iggy, though retired, goes out almost every day.

THE 'INPORT'

St. John's, Canada's 'most colourful city', looks as though it was painted in bold blocks of colour by an abstract artist. Built on a steep hillside above the port, it is a kind of mini-San Francisco.

SAILORS

For five centuries, ships of all nations have visited St. John's. Russians today are among the most numerous visitors.

... AND SANYOS

Like all tourists, they take back treasures they can't buy at home.

SOFT LIGHTS

St. John's has a unique sophistication born of almost 500 years of existence. It's a place where you dine well on traditional seafood or international haute cuisine.

...AND SYMPHONIES

There is an excellent symphony orchestra and flourishing artistic community. Among many festivals, the International Sound Symposium attracts performers and musical creators from around the world. New-foundland also has a living tradition of folk music and is one of the few places where songs are still written as commentaries on current events.

THE BATTERY — OUTPORT IN THE INPORT — The Battery is an old fishing community which winds up and down and around the rocks at the entrance to St. John's harbour. It's a quiet place where fishermen mend nets and swap stories, but their community is changing. Sea-people may now have a doctor, professor, or broadcaster as a neighbour but all are brought together by love of a unique environment. The Battery got its name from guns mounted there which defended the city against many attacks.

REFLECTIONS OF THE FUTURE

Like reflections of 'saltbox' houses in the windows of new tall buildings, an old community has new hopes. In some areas, it has become a world leader.

In tele-medicine, Dr. Max House heads one of the world's most advanced systems which, from its base at Memorial University, routinely practices electronic medicine in the Caribbean and has worked as far away as Kenya.

The man on the screen is a diver on an offshore oil platform with a suspected brain condition. Doctors in St. John's literally looked into his eyes and determined it was only an infection. The patient was reassured and a $5000 emergency helicopter trip was avoided.

Telemedicine uses the facilities of a unique community-service communications network developed to meet the needs of isolated communities. In addition to medical uses, the system is used by residents, speaking English, French, Indian and Eskimo languages, to discuss everything from hunting and fishing to education and sports.

Newfoundland is also a leader in oceanography, fisheries and cold water research, and on icebergs which menace offshore oilfield developments.

A major Earth Sciences Centre has been established because of oil development and because Newfoundland is geologically one of the most interesting places on earth.

GHOSTS — Lamanche, south of St. John's, was largely destroyed by a tidal wave 40 years ago. Today it is one of Newfoundland's many abandoned communities whose people, with government assistance, moved to larger centres. Now houses with empty eyes stare silently out to sea.

HARD ROCK

When They Built Newfoundland
They Built Her To Last!

Newfoundland's rock is as interesting as it is colourful.

The rocks of eastern Newfoundland were once part of North Africa. Those of the west were part of North America and the two were pushed together in a cosmic crunch 400 million years ago.

These rocks are among the oldest in the world and have been through several ice ages. The result is natural sculpture everywhere:

— The Old Man, standing in the bay across from our house at Admiral's Cove. Many boats have sheltered behind him in storms.

— Giants' Bowling balls left by retreating ice.

— Rocks glowing with rainbow colours.

— And cliffs which show the awesome power which has flipped mountainous layers of stone like so many pancakes. At Gros Morne Park, there is the world's best example of a place where the earth has been literally turned inside out.

SOFT ROCK   Newfoundland is known as the Dark and Brooding Rock, but it also has green gentle landscapes, with rolling hills, fields of flowers, and deep, fragrant moss. Sometimes we seemed to be in the west of Ireland.

51

FOUR-LEGGED FRIENDLIES

Even the animals are congenial. Little Newfoundland ponies ran across their pasture for a conversation each time we went walking on the Downs at Ferryland. Once, when we were having a sundowner, a pony helped himself to a glass of sherry. Wonderful friendly! The little horses, many of whom roam the roads freely, are a unique breed similar to those of Sable Island.

CRACKIES

The real Newfoundland dogs are the little "Crackies" found everywhere in contrast to the traditional black Newfoundlands which are now almost rare. With a mixed heritage, Crackies have evolved into a distinct type. They have heart and humour and are busy, busy, busy! A pair on our road patrolled a two mile stretch every day at a full gallop on their stubby little legs pausing only for discussions on where to go next. Tiny, our next door dog, picked blueberries faster than we could but, unfortunately, kept them for himself.

THE WEARIN' OF THE RED

Redheads are everywhere on the Southern Shore in the heart of Irish Newfoundland. The pictures on the opposite page were taken at a single parish garden party. Some colourful!

NEARER TO GOD

The Virgin in a window with the harbour below; and a church on a rock above a fishing stage. These pictures symbolize the position churches continue to occupy in Newfoundland. Living in a harsh environment, often isolated, Newfoundlanders have needed spiritual strength and the churches helped them find it.

GARDEN PARTIES AND TURKEY TEAS

Games, crafts, food and fun. Parish fund-raising is a colourful affair. Father McKenna's crown-and-anchor wager is reflected in his glasses.

JOY!

FRIENDS IN ETERNAL CONVERSATION

THE BLOOMING ROCK

Wildflowers in astonishing abundance give Newfoundland a kaleidoscope of colour from May to November. An almost infinite variety line the roads, fill fields, and cover ponds. Pitcher plants, the provincial flower, brighten the unbarren Barrens (page 58) and even the rocks are alive with lichen and blossoms.

Now turn the page and smell summer!

FLOWING PONDS
AND
FALLING LEAVES

Life in Newfoundland centres around inland waters almost as much as those of the sea. The island is covered by lakes and ponds whose warm waters attract people for swimming, fishing, and holidaying. This is where moose feed, lilies bloom and, in autumn, leaves fall in golden patterns.

PITCHING IN

On small Newfoundland acreages, it doesn't pay to use expensive machinery so the crop comes in with horses, hand-made tools, and high neighbourly humour. Everyone has a hay day!

HAY THERE!

FENCY WORK

Hand-crafted fences zig, zag, and twist through every community. The most interesting are the many varieties made from starrigans, an old Irish word meaning dried saplings. In earlier days, when people depended on vegetable patches for survival, every square foot of arable ground was fenced as protection from free-roaming animals. Today, fences remain the handiest places to dry fishing boots and gloves.

CODFISH,

CANNONS

AND COLONIES

History is almost a living presence in Newfoundland, the place where Canada began.

The story starts with the native people, the Beothucks, who were exterminated by white settlers, a stain on the history of Canada and the English-speaking peoples.

The first white visitors may have been St. Brendan and his crew, the astonishing sea-going Irish monks who crossed the Atlantic in a leather-covered boat in the 6th century.

The first colonization of North America was attempted almost 1000 years ago by the Vikings who established a community at L'Anse au Meadows, on the Strait of Belle Isle, Their sod-house settlement has been imaginatively re-created as a historic site with a museum, exhibitions, and audio-visual presentation. Visitors learn that the Vikings apparently came, not as marauders, but as traders cutting timber, a valuable commodity in Greenland and Iceland. After perhaps a dozen years, they retreated, probably because of native attacks.

The name, L'Anse aux Meadows is a corruption of the French *l'Anse aux Meduses,* cove of jellyfish.

Permanent white settlement began with the Basques who were probably fishing here before Columbus. The French and British came soon after seeking gold and a route to China. They failed but succeeded in establishing a major fishing industry which, in the case of Britain, grew to be her largest overseas enterprise. They established St. John's, the oldest of the British and French cities in the New World, and had built it into an important centre, with iron founderies and ship chandleries, by the time Jacques Cartier arrived in 1534.

By the time Sir Humphrey Gilbert arrived in 1583 to claim Newfoundland and begin the British Empire, St. John's was a major centre, with the harbour filled with ships "of

all nations to the number of 36 sail.'' Sir Humphrey was provided with a house suitable for a distinguished courtier and spent most of his 17 days in St. John's in feasting and entertainment — not quite the image most people have of an intrepid explorer penetrating the wilderness.

St. John's went on to have a colorful and often violent history. Three times it was captured by the French and twice burned and once captured and burned by the Dutch who were then at war with Britain. It was also attacked by pirates and privateers.

The French and Dutch, as well as pirates, also attacked Ferryland, a colony established south of St. John's by Sir George Calvert, later Lord Baltimore. Cannons, used in the defense of Ferryland, are today rusting in the grass and it gives a strange feeling to see them lying where they were abandoned three centuries ago.

Calvert was forced to quit Ferryland when winters turned cold and his wife was no longer able to stand the climate. The family sought better conditions to the south — thus becoming the first Canadians to go south to escape the winter. He was granted a charter to establish the colony of Maryland and the city of Baltimore is named after him.

Leadership in Ferryland was taken over by the astonishing David Kirke. As a privateer commissioned by the British government, Kirke and his brothers blockaded the St. Lawrence River in 1626, captured a French fleet sent to reinforce the Quebec colony, and then captured Quebec itself taking Champlain prisoner. Three years later, Quebec was returned to France under the terms of a peace treaty but Kirke himself was not dislodged for another two years.

Most mainland Canadians are unaware there was a private citizen who became Conqueror of Quebec a century before Wolfe. Every Newfoundlander knows the story.

In the struggle between Britain and France, Newfoundland was a battleground controlled at various times by both sides. The French established a major fortress at Placentia on the south coast which, together with Louisbourg on Cape Breton Island, and Quebec itself, constituted their main line of defense.

Despite war and hardships, settlers continued to arrive, mostly from Ireland and the West of England. Early Irish colonists, who settled near Cape Race at the southeast tip of the island, were abandoned by their leaders when funds ran out. One can imagine their feelings; seeing the leaders sail away leaving them on a rocky shore, in one of the foggiest areas of the world, surrounded by stormy seas and hundreds of miles of Barrens. Although farmers with no sea experience, they somehow survived in one of Newfoundland's many extraordinary stories of endurance.

Although conditions were harsh, the fishing grounds were rich and many Newfoundlanders became well off for their times. Several towns each produced more wealth than all French Canada combined.

The wealthiest of the Newfoundlanders were the Pirate Admirals who lived lives so colourful they are the stuff of fiction. Peter Easton, Newfoundland's favorite hero, outraged Newfoundland commercial interests because, among other sins, he recruited 500 fishermen annually to man his fleet of 10 ships thus disrupting the fishing industry. Business leaders persuaded the British government to send a Royal Navy squadron against Easton but the mission failed when the navy turned pirate and joined Easton. The commander, Henry Mainwaring, took over the pirate fortress at Harbour Grace while the Admiral went on to establish a new stronghold at Ferryland.

Mainwaring, with "eight sail of strong ships, well armed," became rich and powerful, and succeeded in defeating a Spanish naval flotilla specially fitted to do battle with him. He was then invited to return to England where he became a Member of Parliament, was knighted, and finally became a Vice-Admiral and a senior commander of the Royal Navy!

Easton ended his career even more spectacularly, when he captured the Spanish treasure fleet in the Azores in 1614, and then became Marquis of Savoy living in splendour in France — a nation whose ships he had plundered.

Crime sometimes pays!

In modern times, Newfoundland was Marconi's base when he received his historic wireless message from across the Atlantic. It was the base for the first trans-Atlantic air crossing made by Alcock and Brown and for many other famous early flights. In the Second World War, it was the western base for the Battle of the Atlantic convoys and for the Ferry Command flights which sent a stream of warplanes across the ocean. At its height, Ferry Command planes took off at the rate of one every sixty seconds.

Today, in addition to its fishing industry, Newfoundland is a major centre for offshore oil and world-leading research and development in several fields.

This story of Newfoundland is colourful and dramatic but is strangely little known by late-comers who live on the mainland.

BEAUTIFUL WEATHER

Newfoundland has great weather and lots of it.

This is the place where the continent's three main weather routes meet — one sweeping across Canada, another crossing the central United States, and a third coming up the Atlantic seaboard. Weather systems thus converge on Newfoundland like trucks roaring down freeways. Adding to the traffic, the cold Labrador current collides with the warm Gulf Stream just south of the island.

The result:

— High winds, exploding seas, and excitement.

— A great place for wind chimes.

— And fog, beautifully soft and mysterious, provides natural magic shows. It creates illusions as it drifts and lifts. Visions appear and disappear in a fairytale atmosphere, sometimes dark and scary, sometimes bright and luminous. Then, suddenly, it is gone.

— There's rain, but less than in some areas of British Columbia, and it usually doesn't last because the weather is ever-changing. As Newfoundlanders say: "If you don't like the weather, wait 15 minutes!"

— And sunshine, lots of it, clear and sparkling; no pollution.

— Finally, all this weather creates some of the most dramatic skies in the world.

IN THE FOG

Fog is beautiful, shimmering, irridescent; creating never-ending magic shows. At sea, it can cause nightmares but it also creates seascapes with extraordinary drama. This shot was taken en route to Labrador.

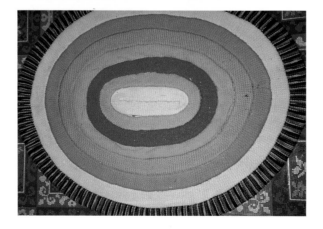

COLOUR-FULL PEOPLE

Something about New-foundland inspires creative people. Colours, contours, and spirit combine to produce outstanding native artists and to attract some of the finest from elsewhere.

Anne Meredith Barry, noted painter and print-maker, is one member of the community.

In fashion, Newfoundland designs sell across North America, some custom-produced for the rich and famous. Gill Campbell, of Woof Design, sells half a million dollars worth of knitwear annually.

Diana Dabinett's creations, such as the underwater scene on silk on the opposite page, sell across Canada.

Iroquois artist Stan Hill Jr. has sold his antler carvings in 13 countries.

Doll-maker Margaret Matthews' creations are found around the world.

Jim Aspell, our wood-working friend and neighbour, is the Puffin King of Admiral's Cove.

Eileen Hartery of Portugal Cove South is typical of the women who have made hooked rugs and sweaters in the outports for centuries.

FOR THE BERRIES!

Bakeapples, partridge berries, cracker berries, blackberries, dogberries, chuckleberries and a hillside of others. Wild berries are part of life in Newfoundland. Pies, tarts, preserves, puddings, cakes, and wines — all part of the heritage. Picking them has long been a family pleasure and eating them, especially the famous partridgeberry pudding, is an essential part of the traditional Sunday dinner.

Berry picking on 'Blueberry Hill', above Admiral's Cove, was a pleasure we enjoyed from August to November. Another treat was discovering Granny Andrew's pastry recipe.

Try it! It's simple, delicious, and never fails!

GERT'S GRANDMOTHERS' BLUEBERRY PIE

Really No-Fail Recipe:

2 cups flour
1/2 cup margarine or butter
1/2 cup shortening or lard
1/4 cup cold water

Cut ingredients together with a pastry cutter or with two knives. When in small pieces, work gently and quickly with fingers into pea-sized pieces. Don't worry if ingredients are not smoothly mixed. There will be bits of butter throughout.

Form ingredients into a ball. Don't be too hard on it. Cut ball in half. Roll out, on lightly-floured cloth or board, into pie-plate-sized circles.

Place one circle in pie-plate and form to fit. Add filling. Add top. Seal edges by pinching pastry together with thumbs. Cut breathing holes in top crust. Bake 45 min. at 400 F.

For Fresh Fruit Pies
Combine half cup sugar and 2 tablespoons flour. Sprinkle 1/2 mixture on bottom crust, fill with fruit, sprinkle remaining mixture on top of fruit before adding top crust.
Enjoy!

LAUGHING

LAUNDRY

Newfoundland Laundry Instructions:

1. Wash and hang
2. Wait for natural rinse cycles to pass through
3. Fluff with fog cycle
4. Then watch it laugh itself dry, dancing in the wind-and-spin cycle.

YE'LL BE WELCOME! A special welcome awaits in the homes of Newfoundland. One mis-directed mainland couple spent the night in a private home thinking it was a bed-and-breakfast. Only in the morning, after having been hospitably breakfasted, did they discover their mistake. "Why would ye be wanting to pay?" the hosts asked. Mrs. Costello's home in Ferryland, a real B&B, is near the site of a pirate admiral's stronghold where cannons often roared.

PARTY ICE

Fall garments gone, the wild wind spray
Gives shore plants new dazzling dresses.
Celebrating the festive season,
The pond becomes a crystal fantasy.

COME-BY-CHANCE
VOLUNTEER
FIRE DEPT.

T.C.H. WEST
HILLVIEW
ST. JONES WITHIN →

SMILING DOWN

DILDO RUN
CAUSEWAY

↑ T.C.H. WEST
HODGE'S COVE →
LITTLE HEARTS EASE →

ROUTE 239
GOOSE COVE

MAIN TICKLE
CAUSEWAY

POST OFFICE
COME BY CHANCE

ROUTE 80
HEARTS DELIGHT

ROUTE 10
WITLESS BAY

CUPIDS

Gin Cove

Paradise
A0A 2E0

Smiling Down The Road

From Come-By-Chance to Paradise,
Newfoundland has some of the most
imaginative placenames in the world.
They send you smiling on your way.

"I looks to ye and I smiles!

— Traditional Irish toast.